Routes of Science

Electricity

Chris Woodford

BLACKBIRCH®
PRESS

THOMSON

GALE

San Diego • Detroit • New York • San Francisco • Cleveland • New Haven, Conn. • Waterville, Maine • London • Munich

THOMSON

GALE

Every effort has been made to trace
the owners of copyrighted material.

PHOTOGRAPHIC CREDITS
Cover: Photodisc (l); Getty/Hulton Archive (t);
Science & Society Picture Library (b).

Corbis: Shelley Gavin 34; **DaimlerChrysler:**
37; **Getty Images:** Hulton Archive 21, 25;
Mary Evans Picture Library: 6, 7, 10, 11t,
11b, 14, 15t, 16t, 18, 20, 23; **Photodisc:** 1,
4–5, 35; **Science & Society Picture Library:**
12, 24tl, 28b, 31; **University of Pennsylvania:**
Smith Image Collection 8, 9bl, 9br, 13, 16b,
24tl, 26, 27, 28t, 30, 31b.

Consultant: Don Franceschetti, Ph.D.,
Distinguished Service Professor,
Departments of Physics and Chemistry,
The University of Memphis,
Memphis, Tennessee

For The Brown Reference Group plc
Text: Chris Woodford
Project Editor: Sydney Francis
Designer: Elizabeth Healey
Picture Researcher: Helen Simm
Illustrators: Darren Awuah,
    Richard Burgess, and Mark Walker
Managing Editor: Bridget Giles
Art Director: Dave Goodman
Children's Publisher: Anne O'Daly
Production Director: Alastair Gourlay
Editorial Director: Lindsey Lowe

LIBRARY OF CONGRESS CATALOGING-IN-PUBLICATION DATA

Woodford, Chris.
 Electricity / by Chris Woodford.
    p. cm. -- (Routes of science)
Includes bibliographical references and index.
Contents: The mysteries of electric fluid – From frogs' legs to batteries – Electricity
meets magnetism – The power of electricity – Electricity makes waves – The
electronic age – Into the future
  ISBN 1-4103-0165-6 (hardback : alk. paper)
  1. Electricity--Juvenile literature. [1. Electricity.] I. Title. II.
Series.

Printed and bound in Singapore
10 9 8 7 6 5 4 3 2 1

CONTENTS

INTRODUCTION

The quest to understand how electricity works has led to some of the most important discoveries and inventions of all time. At first, though, the mysteries of electricity baffled even the most brilliant thinkers.

PEOPLE OFTEN THINK OF electricity as a modern discovery: It is electricity that powers computers, cellular phones, and satellites in space. Yet scientists have known about simple kinds of electricity, such as static electricity, for more than two thousand years. Only in the last two or three hundred years, however, have people understood electricity well enough to put it to use.

During this time, scientists discovered that static electricity, produced when certain substances are rubbed against each other, and current electricity, which flows through wires, are really the same thing. They have also found that magnetism and electricity are related to each other and are part of a much larger phenomenon called electromagnetism. Scientists have figured out how to harness the power

of electricity on a very large scale in big power plants. They have also mastered electricity on a very tiny scale by devising ways to control electrons inside computer circuits. Electrons are microscopic particles that move when electric currents flow.

How people came to understand electricity is a story of both science (understanding how the world works) and technology (using science to solve everyday problems). The great scientists who solved the mysteries of electricity were often also great inventors who were motivated by the idea of making life easier for people. Sometimes scientists came up with important inventions. Sometimes inventors pushed the frontiers of science forward.

No single person discovered electricity. Instead, our modern ideas have been gradually put together over a long period as scientists built on the work of their predecessors. In some ways, science works like a never-ending relay race, as one generation of scientists passes on the baton of knowledge and discovery to the next. Although scientists know much more about electricity today than ever before, there are still many questions that must be answered before electricity can be understood fully.

1 THE MYSTERIES OF ELECTRIC FLUID

Early scientists thought that electricity was a fluid (like water) that flowed from place to place, but they were not sure whether there was one kind of electric fluid or two.

THE STORY OF ELECTRICITY began around 600 B.C. with ancient Greek thinker Thales of Miletus (625–546 B.C.). Thales found that if he rubbed a piece of amber, it would pick up feathers and bits of cork as a magnet would with metal. Around A.D. 77, Roman author (**Pliny the Elder**) wrote

Science and Stories

Pliny the Elder (23–79 A.D.; above) collected ideas about the world in his book *Natural History*, which was one of the first science encyclopedias. It contained not only science as people study it today, but also stories, superstitions, and ideas about magic.

Static Electricity

Static electricity is caused when electricity builds up in one place. If you walk across a nylon carpet, static electricity builds up on your body. If you then touch something metal, such as a faucet, you might feel a sudden electric shock in your finger. That shock is like a very tiny bolt of lightning that carries the static electricity from your body to Earth.

When rubber balloons are rubbed on a woolen sweater, static electricity builds up on their surface. This pushes the balloons apart.

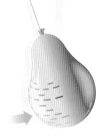

Electric Charge

The amount of electricity something has is called its charge. If you rub a dry plastic rod two or three times, it gains a charge and it can pick up tiny bits of paper. If you rub it ten or twenty times, it gains much more charge and can pick up lots more (or bigger) pieces of paper.

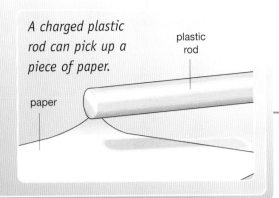

A charged plastic rod can pick up a piece of paper.

plastic rod

paper

about similar simple experiments with electricity in his book *Natural History*. These ancient thinkers had discovered static electricity.

It was not until the seventeenth century that people tried to understand what caused electricity. English doctor and scientist William Gilbert (1544–1603) carried out many experiments on both electricity and magnetism and was the first person to use the word "electricity." Another Englishman, Stephen Gray (1666–1736), found that some materials, such as amber, could hold an electric charge for a long time. Other materials, such as metals, could not store charge at all. This was how Gray discovered the difference between insulators and conductors.

Insulators and Conductors

Insulators are materials like plastic and glass. They hold electricity, which flows through them very poorly or not at all. Conductors are materials, like metal, that do not hold electricity, but carry (conduct) it very well. Electric cables are made from a central wire, which carries the electricity, wrapped in a plastic insulator to keep people from getting electric shocks.

Two Electricities?

Hang a plastic ruler from a cotton thread and rub it a few times with a dry cloth. Now rub another ruler and bring it up to the first one. The two rulers push away from (or repel) one another. If you rub a glass rod and bring it up to the dangling ruler, however, the two pull toward (or attract) one another. An experiment like this one made Charles du Fay think there were two different kinds of electricity, one gained by materials like plastic and another gained by materials like glass.

Watson's Wire

William Watson (1715–1787; left) carried out many experiments on electricity. In one of the most important of these, he showed that electricity could flow down a wire 2 miles (about 3 km) long. The wire stretched through the streets of London, England, and even crossed a bridge over the Thames River.

French chemist Charles François du Fay (1698–1739) thought electricity was caused by (two kinds) of electric fluids. He believed things gained an electric charge when they had more of one kind of electric fluid and less of the other kind. Not everyone believed this idea, however. In 1746, a British scientist named (**William Watson**) suggested that there was only one kind of electric fluid.

Du Fay and Watson had put forward two different theories (ideas suggested by scientists), but which one was correct? Was there one kind of electric fluid or two? (**Benjamin Franklin**) helped settle the issue. During the

1740s, he became fascinated by electricity and even gave up his work so that he would have time to study it. Like Watson, Franklin thought there was just one kind of electric fluid and invented the terms "positive" and "negative" to explain it. Objects that have a lot of electric fluid become negatively charged, while objects that have a little become positively charged. Franklin also proved that lightning is a form of electricity with his famous (kite experiment). This led him to invent the lightning rod, a long piece of metal that runs down the side of tall buildings to protect them from lightning strikes.

Benjamin Franklin

Benjamin Franklin (1706–1790; below) was a distinguished statesman and helped draft the constitution of the United States. He was also an author, publisher, philosopher, and scientist. Apart from the lightning rod, he invented the rocking chair, the wood-burning Franklin stove, and bifocal eyeglasses. In 1770, he discovered the warm Atlantic ocean current called the Gulf Stream.

Flying High

Franklin tried to prove that lightning was a huge electric spark by carrying out a very risky experiment—flying a kite in a thunderstorm. Although the kite and string became charged, no lightning struck the kite. If it had done so, Franklin probably would have been killed!

2 FROM FROGS' LEGS TO BATTERIES

The science of electricity took a dramatic new turn when two Italian scientists discovered that electric charge could be made to flow from one place to another.

BENJAMIN FRANKLIN HAD AN enormous influence on the study of static electricity. This was not only through his own work. During a visit to London, he met English scientist Joseph Priestley (1733–1804) and encouraged him to study electricity. Priestley's work, in turn, spurred on

Henry Cavendish

A millionaire, English scientist Henry Cavendish (1731–1810; left) was nevertheless a shy and shabby figure, eccentrically dressed in a faded violet suit and old-fashioned hat. He loathed women, rarely spoke more than a few words, and seldom appeared in public. Yet his brilliant mind was constantly busy pondering important scientific ideas.

Electric Fields

A magnet creates a powerful but invisible force around it that can attract nearby objects made from certain metals. This is called a magnetic field. In much the same way, an electric charge creates an invisible electric field around itself.

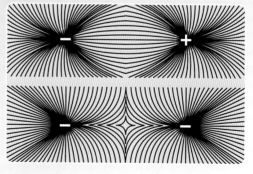

Lines of force spread out from positive (+) and negative (−) electric charges much like the lines of force produced by a magnet. Opposite charges attract and like charges repel each other.

other scientists, notably a Frenchman called Charles Augustin de Coulomb (1736–1806) and the Englishman (**Henry Cavendish**.) Coulomb and Cavendish helped discover how (**electric fields**) work.

Many of the early studies of electricity were made in England, but an Italian physician by the name of (**Luigi Galvani**) made the next major breakthrough. After he studied how electricity could make the muscles of animals jerk, he carried out a series of now-famous (**experiments**) with the legs of dead frogs. Galvani's findings led him to believe (incorrectly) that animals contained "animal electric fluid." He thought this fluid came from the brain and that the flow of fluid caused the muscles to move.

End of the Great Galvani

Luigi Galvani (1737–1798) became a professor at the University of Bologna, Italy, at the age of only 25. A gentle and modest man, he quickly became a distinguished physician and scientist. In 1797 he refused to support Napoléon, the new head of state, and he lost his job, his salary, and his home. He died soon afterward at the age of 61.

Galvani's Experiments

In one of his first electrical experiments, Galvani made a frog's legs twitch by touching them with a pair of scissors during a thunderstorm. He is better known, though, for another experiment (right), when he pushed brass hooks through a frog's legs, hung the legs on an iron railing, and the legs twitched. Galvani thought that animal electricity was responsible for this.

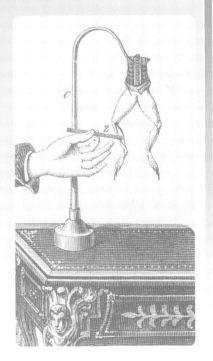

Metals and Batteries

When two different metals are connected using a substance called an electrolyte, electricity is produced. This is the basic idea behind batteries, which were invented by Alessandro Volta. The first battery, known as a voltaic pile, was a sandwich made of alternate disks of silver, disks of cardboard soaked in saltwater (the electrolyte), and disks of zinc.

A copy of the original voltaic pile.

Electric Circuits

When an electric charge builds up in one place, it is called static electricity. When something that has a static charge is connected with a conductor to something that has no charge, the charge flows from the statically charged object to the object with no charge. A flowing charge is known as an electric current or current electricity. Current electricity can also be made to flow continuously around a circular path known as an electric circuit.

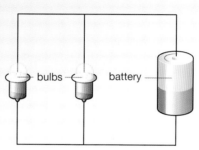

An electric circuit with two bulbs and one battery. The battery produces an electric current that causes the bulbs to light up.

Not everyone believed in animal electric fluid. Another Italian professor, Alessandro Volta (1745–1827), disagreed with Galvani's ideas. After he did experiments with different animals and different metals, he discovered that electricity could be made without animal tissue. Volta believed that an electric charge was produced when two **different metals** touched one another and made an **electric circuit**. Volta called this idea "metallic electricity," but he did not fully settle the question about animal electricity. As a result, some scientists continued to believe Galvani's ideas, and the argument over animal electricity and metallic electricity continued for many years.

Volta's research marked the beginning of a new scientific field called electrochemistry. This is the study of how electricity and chemistry work together. Its most important champion was the English chemist **Humphry Davy**. Davy built batteries that were similar to Volta's, only much bigger, to generate powerful electric currents (flows of electricity). Using a method called **electrolysis,** he passed these currents through chemical compounds and discovered a number of chemical elements, including sodium, potassium, and calcium. Through Davy, Volta's work led to great advances in chemistry.

Humphry Davy

The son of a woodcarver, Humphry Davy (1778–1829; right) is best remembered today for the Davy safety lamp—a device that miners could use without igniting dangerous gases underground. Yet his most important contribution to science was the discovery that electrolysis could split chemical compounds into their component elements.

Electrolysis

In a battery, electricity is produced by two different metals (electrodes) and a chemical (electrolyte) in between them. Electrolysis works in the opposite way. When two electrodes are dipped into a liquid compound (a combination of two or more elements) and a supply of electricity is connected across them, a chemical reaction takes place. This splits the compound into its separate parts. For example, electrolysis can be used to split water into the gases hydrogen and oxygen.

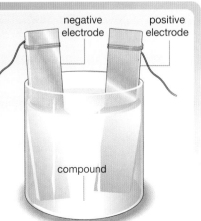

negative electrode

positive electrode

compound

3 ELECTRICITY MEETS MAGNETISM

Electricity and magnetism were once thought to be very different things. During the nineteenth century, scientists discovered that these two phenomena had much more in common than had once been supposed.

THROUGHOUT HISTORY, scientists noted similarities between electricity and magnetism. Ancient Greek philosopher **Thales of Miletus** (*see* page 6) studied both phenomena, as did English scientist **William Gilbert**. Scientists continued to treat electricity and magnetism as though they were

Thales and Magnets

Thales (below) believed magnets had souls because, like people, they were powerful enough to move iron.

The Galileo of Magnetism

William Gilbert (1544–1603) was given the nickname "the Galileo of magnetism" after he published a book that explained how magnets work. Gilbert was the first to suggest that Earth behaves like a giant magnet. He thought this explained why compass needles always point north. He was right.

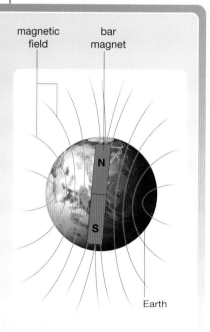

magnetic field   bar magnet

Earth

Like a bar magnet, Earth has a magnetic field with north (N) and south (S) poles.

separate things until the start of the nineteenth century.

One of the first people to suggest that there might be a link between electricity and magnetism was Italian philosopher and lawyer Gian Domenico Romagnosi (1761–1835). Around 1802, Romagnosi experimented with a Voltaic pile (*see* page 12) and a magnetic needle. The results of his experiments did not attract much attention because they were published in a little-known newspaper. The definite link between electricity and magnetism was made by Danish physicist **Hans Christian Ørsted** (1777–1851) almost twenty years later. Ørsted became famous for his discovery; Romagnosi is now largely forgotten.

Ørsted's Experiment

Ørsted first predicted the magnetic effect of an electric current in 1813, but it was not until the winter of 1819–1820 that he proved his theory. In a very simple experiment, He ran a metal wire underneath a compass needle. When he connected the wire to a battery and turned on the current, the compass needle flicked slightly before returning to its original position. The same thing happened when Ørsted switched off the current. He concluded that the electric current produced a magnetic field and it was this field that made the compass needle move.

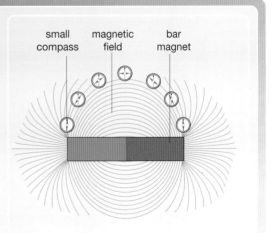

small compass   magnetic field   bar magnet

A compass needle will move as shown above when moved around a bar magnet. Ørsted proved that an electric current has the same effect.

Mathematical Genius

Although largely self-taught, André-Marie Ampère (1775–1836; right) was a gifted child who, by the age of 12, had mastered all the mathematical knowledge then known. He became a math teacher at the age of 21, professor of physics and chemistry at 26, and professor of mathematics eight years later.

By September 1820, news of Ørsted's discovery had traveled to Paris, France. Math professor **André-Marie Ampère** immediately seized upon it. Over the next seven years, Ampère developed a detailed mathematical theory of electricity and magnetism. During his research, he discovered that if two wires carrying electric currents are placed close together, they will attract or repel one another because of the magnetism they produce. Ampère also invented the ammeter for measuring electric current.

An ammeter is a bit like a compass that can measure the size of an electric current. Inside an ammeter, a current passes through a coil of wire. The wire rotates between the poles of a magnet. This makes the needle rotate according

Faraday, Davy's Greatest Discovery

Michael Faraday (1791–1867; right) started life as a poor blacksmith's son who sometimes had to survive a whole week on a single loaf of bread. At the age of 14, he found work as an assistant to a bookbinder. When he got the chance to attend the lectures of Sir Humphry Davy, Faraday took notes, bound them, and sent a copy to Davy. Some time later, Davy gave Faraday a job as his laboratory assistant, taught him chemistry, and helped him become one of the greatest scientists of the nineteenth century.

Generator and Motor

If an electric conductor is moved through a magnetic field, electric current will flow in the conductor. In an electric generator, a conductor such as a coil of wires is moved through a magnetic field made by magnets. This causes current to flow in the wires. In an electric motor, the electric current from a battery or other power source makes a coil of metal into an electromagnet. When placed between two magnets, the coil will turn because of the repelling force of opposing magnetic poles. A device called a commutator reverses the current every half turn to keep up the rotation. The continuous turning motion of the coil drives the motor.

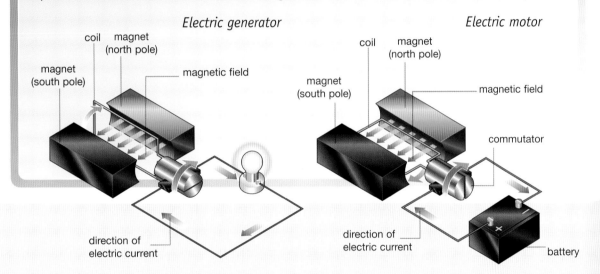

Electric generator   *Electric motor*

to the strength of the current. The size of a current is measured in scientific units called amps (short for amperes), named for Ampère.

Ørsted had proved that electricity could make magnetism. About ten years later, self-taught British scientist Michael Faraday showed the opposite effect: magnetism could be used to make electricity. Faraday also showed how electricity and magnetism could work together to produce a pushing force. With these two discoveries, Faraday developed the basic science that later led to two important inventions: the electric generator and motor.

A Brilliant Mind

When James Clerk Maxwell (1831–1879; left) was a young boy, his tutor claimed he was dull and slow at learning. Nothing could have been farther from the truth. Maxwell had a brilliant mind and a superb memory. He published his first scientific paper at the age of only 14 and entered college at age 16. His outstanding scientific career has been compared in importance with those of the great scientists Sir Isaac Newton and Albert Einstein. Maxwell devoted the last five years of his life to publishing the scientific notebooks of an earlier genius of electricity, Henry Cavendish (*see* page 10.)

Scottish physicist (**James Clerk**

Maxwell) turned Faraday's results into a complete theory that linked electricity and magnetism. Maxwell's theory explained everything scientists had found out about both electricity and magnetism—from the way Thales could pick up feathers with his charged piece of amber to Faraday's demonstration of the electric generator and motor.

Maxwell's theory is called "electromagnetism" and is based on four mathematical (**equations**.) Electromagnetism explains that electricity and magnetism are really two different aspects of the same phenomenon, like the head and the tail of the same animal. Both electric charges and magnetic poles (the ends of a magnet) can create an electromagnetic field that stretches out all around them.

Maxwell secured a reputation as a great scientist with his theory of electromagnetism. Apart from this, he also made a number of other important contributions to physics.

Maxwell published important work on optics (the study of light) and the theory of how gases store heat energy. As a young scientist still in his 20s, he developed a theory that the rings around the planet Saturn were made of small, separate particles. This theory was proved to be correct more than one hundred years later by a Voyager space probe.

Maxwell's Equations

In 1873, Maxwell published his theory of electromagnetism. It was a brilliant piece of science in which he summed up the entire science of electricity and magnetism in just four equations. Using complex math, Maxwell's equations describe how an electric charge creates an electric field, while the poles of a magnet create a magnetic field. The equations also show that a changing electrical field can produce magnetism and a changing magnetic field can produce electricity.

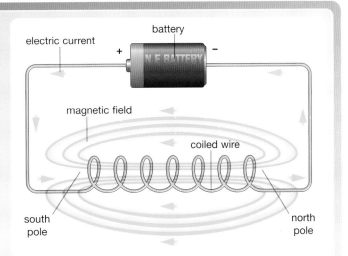

When an electric current flows through a coil of wire, it creates a magnetic field all around it. The field has a north pole and a south pole—just like a bar magnet. This electromagnetic phenomenon is explained completely by Maxwell's equations.

4 THE POWER OF ELECTRICITY

Until the nineteenth century, electricity was little more than a curiosity for scientists to study. When ingenious inventors discovered how to harness its power, the age of electricity truly began.

BEFORE THE 1800s, PEOPLE HAD no idea what electricity could be used to do. The crucial scientific breakthrough that brought about the age of electricity was made around the

Joule's Obsession

Unlike many scientists, James Prescott Joule (above) did not work at a university. As a wealthy man with a large private income, he funded his own research. Joule was so obsessed by energy that he even carried out energy experiments during his honeymoon. He kept his own steam engine at home for his research but had to get rid of it when the neighbors complained!

Resistance

Conductors such as metals allow current to flow through them easily. They resist the flow of electricity very little, so they are said to have low electrical resistance. It is harder to make a current flow through insulators such as wood or plastic. These are said to have a high resistance. The theory of resistance was originally developed in the 1820s by German physicist Georg Simon Ohm (1787–1854).

The voltage produced by the battery in both cases is the same, but a more powerful resistor allows less current to flow through the circuit.

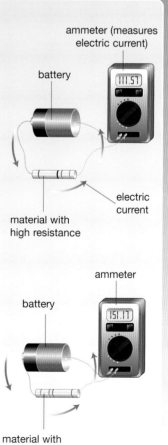

ammeter (measures electric current)

battery

electric current

material with high resistance

ammeter

battery

material with low resistance

middle of the nineteenth century by Scottish physicist (**James Prescott Joule**) (1818–1889). Joule proved that electricity is a type of energy, just like heat or light. In the 1830s, he carried out an experiment with electricity and heat. When he published his results in 1840, he showed how the (**resistance**) of an electric circuit could be used to turn a certain amount of electrical energy into the same amount of heat energy.

In the years that followed, Joule performed more work with energy. He became famous when he proved that one form of energy can be converted into exactly the same amount of a different type of energy. This important finding became known as the (**conservation of energy**).

Conservation of Energy

The theory of energy conservation explains that energy cannot be created out of thin air or made to disappear completely—it can only be turned into other forms of energy. In other words, energy is always conserved (maintained). For example, when a moving automobile screeches to a halt, most of the kinetic (movement) energy that it had is converted into heat energy—the brakes heat up when the automobile slows down. In this illustration, power from a battery (**1**) is used to heat water into steam (**2**). The steam provides kinetic energy that turns a turbine (**3**). That kinetic energy is changed into electrical energy by a generator. Electrical energy can be used to power devices such as lightbulbs (**4**), sound systems (**5**), and electric heaters (**6**).

5 sound system (sound energy)

6 electric bar heater (heat energy)

4 lightbulb (light energy)

3 turbine and generator (electrical energy)

2 steam (kinetic energy)

1 battery (chemical energy)

Electric motors provide an example of a way in which electricity can be turned into a useful form of power, because motors convert electrical energy into mechanical energy that can drive machines. Although the basic science behind motors was demonstrated by Michael Faraday, practical motors really developed through the work of British inventor **William Sturgeon.** Sturgeon developed the first practical **electromagnet** in 1825 by wrapping a length of wire many times around a piece of iron shaped like a horseshoe. When he passed an electric current through this device, Sturgeon found it could pick up pieces of metal up to twenty times its own weight. He also used an electromagnet as the main

William Sturgeon

Born to a life of grinding poverty, William Sturgeon (1783–1850) ran away to join the army. As a cadet, he taught himself science and made kites that could give people electric shocks. His claim to fame was the invention of the commutator, a device that allows an electric motor to rotate continuously in the same direction by reversing the electric current twice each time the motor turns around (*see* page 17.)

Build an Electromagnet

An electromagnet is a magnet made by electricity. It is very easy to build your own. Take one 1.5-volt battery, about 12 inches (30 cm) of plastic-covered wire, and a thick metal nail. Wrap the cable tightly around the nail to make a coil. Connect the ends of the cable to the battery using clips or sticky tape. Try to pick up paper clips or other small pieces of metal with your magnet.

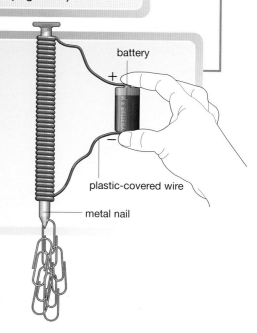

battery

plastic-covered wire

metal nail

The Electric Weather Forecast

America's great nineteenth-century physicist Joseph Henry (1797–1878) made many important contributions to science. In 1846, he became the first director of the Smithsonian Institution, where he began to make detailed observations of the weather. One of the first uses of Henry's electric telegraph was to transmit weather forecasts. This work eventually led to the formation of the U.S. Weather Bureau.

component of his electric motor, which he invented in 1832.

Sturgeon was not the only scientist interested in motors. (Joseph Henry) greatly advanced their development by showing how it is possible to make much more powerful electromagnets (and thus electric motors) using large coils of fine wire. In the 1830s, he made a massive electromagnet for Yale University that could lift 2,086 pounds (946 kg); Sturgeon's electromagnet had been able to lift only 9 pounds (4 kg). Henry also demonstrated how electromagnets could be used to send information by building the first practical (electrical telegraph.)

Disability and Determination

Edison's deafness was one of the reasons he worked so hard. Apart from giving him a reason to prove himself, it spurred on a number of his inventions, including the improvements he made to the electrical telegraph. Edison (below) was someone for whom disability was no barrier to great achievement.

The Fight over Light

English chemist and engineer Joseph Wilson Swan (1828–1914) claimed to have invented the lightbulb in the 1870s, at about the same time as Thomas Edison. At first, Edison and Swan argued over who had invented the lamp. Later, they joined forces and set up a company together to profit from the invention.

Swan's lightbulb (left) and Edison's lightbulb (right).

One man is remembered more than any other for moving the world into the age of electricity: Thomas Alva Edison (1847–1931). While he was still very young, **Edison** started to have problems with his hearing. This meant he found it difficult to hear his teachers in school. Instead, he turned to books as his main source of learning.

One of Edison's first inventions was an improved version of the electrical telegraph. He went on to develop microphones, experimental electric railroads, movie cameras, and the invention for which he is best known —the **electric lightbulb**. Often described as a **genius**, he received nearly 1,100 patents (exclusive rights to one's inventions) in his lifetime.

Electric inventions would have been little use to people without a supply of electricity to power them. Here, too, Edison proved himself to be a pioneer. In 1882, he built a prototype power plant to generate electricity in London, England. Later the same year, Edison constructed the world's first permanent power plant on Pearl Street in New York City. Both of these plants produced electricity using coal-powered steam engines to drive large electric generators.

Although Edison played a key role in the development of electricity, he was much more of an inventor than a scientist. He was more concerned with making useful things than with finding out how those things actually worked.

Genius or Workaholic?

When people said Edison was a genius, he replied: "Genius is one percent inspiration and ninety-nine percent perspiration." By this he meant that hard work and determination are often much more important to scientists and inventors than a brilliant mind. Edison liked work more than anything else—so much so that his family complained about how much time he spent in his laboratory.

5 ELECTRICITY MAKES WAVES

Toward the end of the nineteenth century, scientists realized that electricity and magnetism could travel through space in the form of waves. This led rapidly to the development of radio and television.

THE ANCIENT GREEKS SAW electricity as static: something that stayed in one place. Galvani, Volta, and those who followed them showed that electricity could also flow down wires in the form of an electric current (*see* pages 10–13). (Michael Faraday) went even further and suggested electricity and magnetism could travel through space in waves.

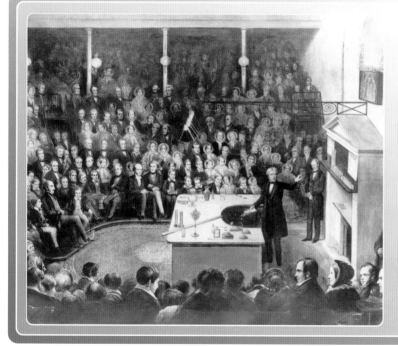

Faraday's Vibrations

From the seventeenth century onward, scientists saw electricity as an invisible fluid that flowed from one place to another like water. In a public lecture in 1846, Faraday proposed that electricity actually moved through conductors in waves, or what he called "ray vibrations" (shaking movements).

Electromagnetic Radiation

Light, radio waves, and X rays are all types of electromagnetic radiation that travel in waves at the speed of light. The different types of radiation are arranged on a spectrum (right) according to wavelength, starting with longest and lowest-energy wavelengths (radio waves) and moving up to the shortest and highest-energy wavelengths (gamma rays, such as from a nuclear explosion). Wavelength is the distance between the peaks or the troughs of a wave.

wave   peak

trough

wavelength

ELECTROMAGNETIC SPECTRUM

"mushroom" cloud

gamma rays

X rays

ultraviolet light

visible light

infrared rays (heat)

microwaves

radio waves

Building on Faraday's work, James Clerk Maxwell calculated the speed of these waves and found it was virtually the same as the speed of light. This made Maxwell think that light must be carried through the air by electromagnetism. He also theorized that there were other types of (**electromagnetic radiation**) that move at the speed of light.

In 1888, nine years after Maxwell's death, German physicist (**Heinrich Rudolf Hertz**) produced electromagnetic radio waves (the longest wavelengths of electromagnetic radiation) in his laboratory. With careful experiments, Hertz measured the length and frequency of the waves.

Hertz and Frequency

Heinrich Hertz (1857–1894) gave his name to the hertz, a unit of frequency usually written Hz. The frequency of a wave is the number of complete waves that move past a given point in one second. An FM radio broadcast with a frequency of 100 MHz (one hundred million hertz) is carried by waves that arrive at the radio at a rate of one hundred million per second.

Oliver Lodge

Oliver Lodge (1851–1940; left) is famous for inventing a device that could pick up radio signals traveling through air. He also believed people could pick up signals from the dead, and devoted much of his time to researching the paranormal. After his son died in World War I (1914–1918), Lodge spent a lot of time trying to contact him through spiritual mediums.

He showed that radio waves could reflect (bounce off things) and refract (appear to bend through things) much like light, and that they traveled at the same speed as light.

Through his research, Heinrich Hertz discovered that electricity, or electromagnetic radiation, could be transmitted through the air without the need for wires. This proved to be a technological breakthrough as well as a scientific one, because it suggested that information might be carried from place to place in new ways.

In 1894, distinguished British physicist (Oliver Lodge) demonstrated a piece of electrical equipment called a coherer. This device made it possible to detect electromagnetic waves traveling in the air. An Italian named Guglielmo

How Radio Works

Radio carries information invisibly through the air using electromagnetic waves. At a radio station, speech or music is turned into electrical signals by a microphone. These signals are then converted into radio waves. A powerful transmitter beams the waves out in all directions through a large antenna. Smaller antennas inside peoples' radios pick up the waves and turn them back into electrical signals. Finally, a loudspeaker turns the electrical signals back into speech or music.

An early radio wave detector called a Marconi coherer.

Marconi (1874–1937) took this invention much further. Marconi had become interested in radio waves at the age of 20 when he read an obituary of Heinrich Hertz. With homemade equipment, he soon managed to send radio signals over a distance of 1.5 miles (2.4 km). The Italian government was not interested in helping him develop the invention, so he moved to England. There, he went on to develop equipment that could send and receive information without wires over **long distances.** Marconi had invented the wireless, now better known as radio. When radio waves were used to carry pictures through the air as well as sound, television was born.

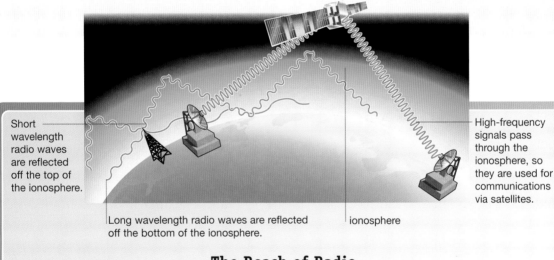

Short wavelength radio waves are reflected off the top of the ionosphere.

High-frequency signals pass through the ionosphere, so they are used for communications via satellites.

Long wavelength radio waves are reflected off the bottom of the ionosphere.

ionosphere

The Reach of Radio

In 1901, Marconi succeeded in sending radio signals across the Atlantic from Cornwall, England, to St. John's, Newfoundland. Many people had refused to believe this was possible, because they thought Earth's curved surface would make the waves fly off into space. In fact, there is an electrically charged layer of Earth's atmosphere called the ionosphere, which acts like a huge curved mirror, and reflects electromagnetic radio signals back to Earth. Earth in turn reflects the radio waves back to the ionosphere, and so on. In this way, radio waves can zigzag around the world, and the ionosphere makes it possible to pick up radio stations on the other side of Earth.

6 THE ELECTRONIC AGE

At the turn of the twentieth century, physicists discovered new particles called electrons, which seemed to carry electricity. This discovery led to the age of microelectronics and computers.

DESPITE EVERYTHING SCIENTISTS had learned about electricity by the end of the nineteenth century, they remained puzzled about electricity's causes. Was there one single thing behind electricity, or different things that caused static electricity, current electricity, and electromagnetism?

In 1874, Irish physicist George Johnstone Stoney (1826–1911)

Electron Theory

The electron theory explains that both static electricity and current electricity are made by electrons. Static electricity is produced when electrons collect in one place. Electrons have a tiny negative charge, so a negatively charged object must have gained extra electrons. Similarly, a positively charged object must have lost electrons. Current electricity is caused when electrons move along a cable, carrying their tiny charges with them.

Clumsy Thomson?

Despite his brilliant mind, John Joseph Thomson (1856–1940; below) was very clumsy with his hands. His assistants encouraged him not to touch his experiments, and his wife did not let him do jobs around the house!

(*see* page 32.)

Discovering the Electron

Thomson used a large glass bulb with a metal plate (or cathode) inside that was heated until it gave off rays. Thomson showed that these rays could be bent by electric or magnetic fields, which meant they must have an electric charge. He suggested that cathode rays were really microscopic particles. Thomson argued (correctly) that each particle (now known to be electrons) carried a small negative charge and must be present in every atom (*see* page 32.)

Thomson's original cathode ray tube.

suggested that there must be a tiny building block of electricity out of which bigger charges were made. Seven years later, German physicist Hermann von Helmholtz (1821–1894) argued that there were particles of electricity. Stoney went on to propose that electric current was really the movement of these small particles, each of which had a tiny charge. Stoney named these particles "electrons" in 1891. The following year, Dutch physicist Hendrik Antoon Lorentz (1853–1928) helped turn these ideas into the **electron theory** of electricity.

All that remained was to prove electrons really existed. In 1897, British physicist **J. J. Thomson** discovered the electron when he was experimenting with **cathode rays.**

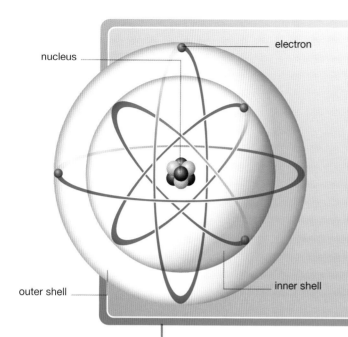

nucleus

electron

outer shell

inner shell

Inside the Atom

Shortly after his discovery of the electron, Thomson suggested that atoms are like plum puddings, with negatively charged electrons (plums) randomly dotted around positively charged matter (the pudding). Scientists now know that atoms are really made up of a central core of positive matter (the nucleus) around which electrons revolve (left).

Thomson's important find helped scientists unravel the mystery of the **atom.** It also helped to reveal the connection between electricity and electrons. This laid the foundations for a whole new technology—electronics.

The modern **electronic** age really began in 1906 when U.S. inventor Lee De Forest (1873–1961) invented the triode vacuum tube. This device could either amplify (make larger) tiny electric currents or switch them on and off. This ability to boost weak electrical signals later led to much improved radio sets and televisions. De Forest later became known as "the father of radio."

Vacuum tubes were also used in early computers until the 1940s, when three U.S. physicists, **John Bardeen,** Walter Brattain (1902–1987), and William Shockley (1910–1989),

Electric or Electronic?

Electrical appliances are simple things powered by electricity, such as lamps and stoves. Electronic appliances are usually more complex devices, such as radios, TVs, and computers. In an electrical appliance, electricity provides nothing more than power; in electronic equipment, electricity also controls how the appliance works. The most sophisticated types of electronic equipment, such as computers, use electrons to store and process numbers (digits). This is termed digital electronics.

invented the transistor. This was a much better amplifier and switch than the vacuum tube: It was smaller, used less power, and was much more reliable. In the 1950s, U.S. physicists Jack St. Clair Kilby (born 1923) and Robert Noyce (1927–1990) figured out how to squeeze hundreds and later thousands of transistors onto a tiny chip of silicon called an integrated circuit. The next step was the single-chip computer, invented in 1969 by Ted Hoff (born 1937). It was this invention—the microchip—that led to the modern age of palm computers, digital watches, cellular phones, and many other compact electronic devices.

John Bardeen

Brilliant U.S. physicist John Bardeen (1908–1991) is so far the only person to have won the prestigious Nobel prize twice for the same subject. He shared the 1956 prize for physics with Brattain and Shockley. In 1972, he won the physics prize again with Leon Cooper and J. Robert Schrieffer for the theory of superconductivity. That theory explains how some materials can conduct electricity without resistance at very low temperatures.

7 INTO THE FUTURE

Scientists still have much to learn about electricity and magnetism. Technologists and inventors, meanwhile, are constantly discovering new ways of putting the science of electromagnetism to use.

ALTHOUGH THE DISCOVERY OF the electron was important, there is much still to be discovered about the nature of electricity and the way electrons behave.

In one major area of research, physicists have been trying to find out how the force that controls electromagnetism relates to the other three (**fundamental forces**)

Four Forces

Four fundamental forces are believed to control the whole of nature: the electromagnetic force responsible for all electric and magnetic phenomena, the strong nuclear force that holds atoms together, the weak nuclear force that controls radioactivity, and the force of gravity that holds the planets in orbit around the Sun.

Richard P. Feynman

One of the most colorful characters of modern physics, Richard P. Feynman (1918–1988) sometimes played conga drums during the lectures he gave. He shared the 1965 Nobel prize for physics for the QED theory. Just before he died, he played a major role in explaining the *Challenger* space shuttle explosion, which killed seven astronauts in 1986.

Lightning and Global Warming

Physicists at Massachusetts Institute of Technology (MIT) are studying global warming by measuring how many times lightning strikes around the world. Global warming is thought to increase the irregularity of the weather and make lightning more common, so this data could provide valuable evidence of how fast Earth is warming up.

Conducting Plastic

Plastics are inexpensive to make, but they do not usually conduct electricity. Although plastics are useful for making electrical insulation, metals—which tend to be expensive—must be used to make electrical components. All that may soon be about to change. The 2000 Nobel prize for chemistry was won by a team of scientists who showed how a new type of plastic could be made to conduct electricity. The discovery could lead to much cheaper computer components.

of nature. One of the most important developments in this area was the theory of quantum electrodynamics (QED), put forward in the 1940s by U.S. physicist Richard P. Feynman. This theory explains how electrons behave when they move around inside electromagnetic fields.

The science of electricity often still offers up surprises. Two hundred years after Benjamin Franklin's kite experiment, physicists continue to discover new things about lightning, for example. Even the idea that insulators do not conduct electricity had to be revised in 2000 with the invention of a new type of plastic.

35

Superconductivity

In 1908, Danish physicist Heike Kamerlingh Onnes (1853–1926) found that some materials lose their electrical resistance if they are cooled down to very low temperatures approaching absolute zero (–459 °F or –273 °C, theoretically the lowest temperature that can ever be reached). This makes them much better carriers of electricity, or superconductors.

Maglev Tains

Unlike conventional trains, which rest on the track as they move and are slowed by friction, magnetic levitation (maglev) trains hover above the track, or rail, suspended by a magnetic field created by powerful electromagnets.

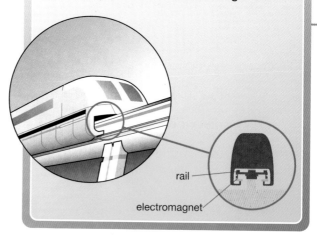

rail

electromagnet

Ever since the discovery of (superconductivity) in 1908, scientists have tried to develop materials that conduct electricity without resistance at higher temperatures. In 1986, high-temperature superconductors were invented that could bring the benefits of superconductivity at more easily reachable temperatures. These are likely to prove useful in faster computers and high-speed (maglev) trains that float along their tracks at up to 300 mph (480 kph).

Developments such as these aim to make electricity a more useful part of everyday life. Electricity may also prove useful in another way: protecting our fragile planet from environmental problems such as pollution and global warming (the way Earth is believed to be getting warmer when people use fossil fuels such as oil and coal). One solution to these problems may be to develop very efficient (**fuel cells**) that make clean electricity from hydrogen gas.

Although electricity has brought enormous benefits for humankind, there are some concerns that electromagnetic radiation could harm people's (**health**). Many scientists are currently trying to find out whether electricity is really as safe as it seems.

With so much research still being conducted and so much still to discover, one thing is clear: The story of electricity has only just begun!

Fuel Cells

A fuel cell is a bit like a battery that never goes dead. It uses a continuous supply of fuel (usually hydrogen gas pumped in from a tank) to make electricity from a chemical reaction. Fuel cells have been used in spacecraft, but they are still too expensive for use in most automobiles and homes.

This modern bus is powered not by a conventional diesel engine but by a fuel cell.

Health Scare?

Cellular phones, high-voltage power lines, and electrical appliances give off electromagnetic radiation. Some people believe that this could cause serious illness including leukemia, although no evidence of this has yet been found. The World Health Organization launched a major project to study this problem in 1996 and is expected to publish its results in 2007.

Glossary

ampere The standard unit for measuring electrical current.

amplify To increase the height of a wave, such as a radio wave.

atom The smallest part of an element that can exist. It is made up of protons and neutrons in a nucleus, surrounded by orbiting electrons.

battery A device that can store electricity using chemical energy.

charge The amount of electricity something contains.

circuit The path around which electric current flows.

compound A substance made of two or more elements.

conductor A material that allows electricity to flow through it very easily.

current electricity The movement of electrical charge through a circuit.

electric shock A sudden jolt or tingling sensation when electricity flows through a person's body.

electrolysis A method of splitting up substances into their component chemical elements using electricity.

electrolyte A liquid, such as that in a battery, which can conduct electricity and be separated by electrolysis.

electromagnet A temporary magnet produced using an electric current.

electromagnetic radiation A wave of electricity and magnetism that travels at the speed of light.

electromagnetism The combined theory of electricity and magnetism.

electron A tiny negatively charged particle inside an atom that carries electricity.

electronics The study of electrons and how they work in electric circuits.

element A substance that cannot be split into two or more different parts by a chemical reaction.

energy The property of an object that gives it the ability to work against forces.

experiment A test of a scientific theory usually carried out in a laboratory.

field The spreading out of electromagnetic effects into the space surrounding electric charges and magnets.

filament A wire that heats up and gives off light when electricity flows through it.

force A pushing or pulling action that causes a change in an object's motion or shape.

generator A device that turns mechanical energy into electricity.

insulator A material that conducts electricity poorly or not at all.

ionosphere An electrically charged part of Earth's atmosphere that bounces or reflects radio waves around the planet.

molecule A group of two or more atoms that unite to form a chemical unit.

motor A device that converts electricity into mechanical energy.

negative charge An electric charge created when electrons are gained.

positive charge An electric charge created when electrons are lost.

resistance The way a material tries to stop an electric current flowing through it.

static electricity A build up of electric charge in one place.

superconductor A material that loses its electrical resistance when it is cooled to an extremely low temperature.

theory A scientific explanation of why something works.

transistor An electronic device that can switch currents on and off or amplify them.

For More Information

BOOKS

Roger Francis Bridgman. *Eyewitness Electronics.* New York: Dorling Kindersley, 2000.

Steve Parker. *Eyewitness Electricity.* New York: Dorling Kindersley, 2000.

Alexandra Parsons. *Electricity: Make it Work.* Princeton, NJ: Two-Can, 2000.

Chris Woodford. *Science Activities: Electricity and Magnetism.* Danbury, CT: Grolier, 2002.

WEBSITES

Boston Museum of Science: Theater of Electricity

A description of some classic experiments from the history of electricity.

www.mos.org/sln/toe/toe.html

Energy Arcade

A virtual tour of a power plant, including 3D models and activities.

www.sdge.com/Arcade/er_0.html

Science Made Simple: Static Electricity

A simple explanation of static electricity.

www.sciencemadesimple.com/static.html

Snacks About Magnetism

Some simple electricity and magnetism experiments you can do at home or at school.

www.exploratorium.edu/snacks/iconmagnetism.html

Yahooligans Electricity Websites

A useful list of sites about electricity.

www.yahooligans.com/Science_and_Nature/Physical_Sciences/Energy/Electricity

Index